NAIL BRUSH, TAPE, SRL GEL, EYE DROPS, ANTI-MOSQUITO STUFF, CITY SHOES, THIN T-SHIRTS, SKIRT, TRIPOD, JACKET. BRING FROM EGYPT TO SUDAN (2003): WATER BAG, BINOCULARS, ZIPPERS FOR BAGS, CUP-A-SOUP, MILK MEDICINE, SECOND SKIN, EYE DROPS, DICTIONARY ENGLISH-ARABIC, LIST SUDANESE W VIDEO CAMERA, SWEDISH SHIRT AND SWEATER, MUG AND SPOON, PHOTOGRAPHERS JAC PACK LIST NETHERLANDS: MAP OF CAIRO, GUIDE BOOK EGYPT, LITERATURE NOMAD BOOK, DICTIONARY ENGLISH-ARABIC, COPY BOOK, MAPS OF EGYPT, MAPS OF SUDAN, PE KNOTS, POEMS, PHILOSOPHY TEXTS, SKETCH BOOK, NOTE BOOKS, DIARY, ADDRESSES EGYPT AND SUDAN, FAMILY PICTURES AND DESERT PICTURES, PORT FOLIO, DATA ARTIC ON CAMEL DISEASES, KEYS OF MY BAGS, PICTURES FOR OFFICIAL PAPERS, COPIES O PERS AND PASSPORT AND VISA, PERMITS, BUY DESERT MAPS, LIST WITH ASSIGNMENTS, CONTACT ADDRESSES, READING GLASSES, EXTRA SET READING GLASSES, CELL PHONE + SIM CARD EGYPT AND SUDAN, PASSPORT, VISA, LETTERS EMBASSY AND MINISTRY OF TOURISM, CREDIT CARD, BANK CARD, CODES, PASSWORDS, EMAIL ADDRESSES, EGYPTIAN MONEY, SUDANESE MONEY, EURO'S, AMERICAN DOLLARS, PURSE, MONEY BELT, EXPENSE FORMS, COMPASS (2X), WATCH, TORCH AND EXTRA TORCH, BATTERIES AA + AAA + LIGHT METER + CAMERAS+ WATCH, MINI DISC RECORDER SONY, ADAPTER, MINI DISCS, MICROPHONE, HEAD PHONES, LAPTOP, ADAPTER, CD'S, DVD'S, BACK UP, ALARM, BINOCULARS, LIGHTER, MATCHES, POCKET KNIFE, SCISSORS, SUNGLASSES, WATER BOTTLES, CONTAINER FOR FUEL COOKER, PLASTIC BAGS IN DIFFERENT SIZES, ZIP LOCK BAGS, ROPE SOFT, SMALL, BIG, EAR PLUGS, CAMERA'S, CAMERA LENSES, UV-FILTER, POLAROID-FILTER, FILM 50, 100, 200, 400 ASA, LENS CLEANER, BACK PACK CAMERA EQUIPMENT, SUITCASE, BATTERIES, LIGHT METER, MANUAL CAMERA AND RECORDER, GREY CARD, POLAROID FILM, STICKERS, NOTE BOOK, GAFFER TAPE, SCREEN, TRIPODS, NOTES, MUESLI, CANDY, CHEWING GUM, TEA, COCOA, MILK POWDER, HERBS, SPICES, SAUCES, DRIED FRUITS, DRIED VEGETABLES, SOUPS, PARMESAN, YELLOW CHEESE, PLASTIC CONTAINERS DIFFERENT SIZES, ARNICA, RSL GEL, PAIN KILLER, COTTON, ANTI-BIOTIC, DESINFECTION SOAP, SECOND SKIN, DAY CREAM, SUNTAN LOTION, HIRSCHTALG CREAM TO PREVENT BLISTERS, MALARIA TABLETS, SCISSORS, AFTER SUN GEL, NIVEA, SUN BLOCK, TAPE, PLASTERS, EYE DROPS, VITAMIN PILLS, INJECTION NEEDLES FOR CAMELS, IVOMEC, TOOTH PASTE, TOOTH BRUSH, MIRROR, MAKE-UP, EAR RINGS, SHAMPOO, HAIR CONDITIONER, SCISSORS HAIR CUT, SCRUB, SAFETY PINS, NEEDLES, COOKER, JERRY CAN FUEL, SLEEPING BAG, SLEEPING MAT, REPAIR SET, ROPES, ZIPPERS FOR BAGS, SMALL BACK PACK, SHOULDER BAG CITY AND EXPEDITION, SADDLE BELTS, NEEDLE TO REPAIR CANVAS BAGS, SADDLE PARTS, JERRY CANS, BUCKET, TOWEL, BLANKET, SHEET, PLATE, MUG, SPOON, SHAWL HEAD, SHAWL NECK, GLOVES, WOOLEN HAT, SHOES CITY, WALKING SHOES, SLIPPERS, TROUSER, JOGGING TROUSERS, SWEAT SHIRT, T-SHIRTS WITH LONG SLEEVES, T-SHIRTS WITH SHORT SLEEVES, SHORTS, JELLABYA, COTTON TROUSERS LOOSE, FLEECE TROUSERS, SKIRT, DRESS, JEANS, BATHING SUIT, SOCKS COTTON THIN AND THICK, SUN HAT, THERMO UNDERWEAR, DOWN JACKET, PRESENTS FOR NOMADS, DROSTE CHOCOLATES FOR CAROL ANN, WARM CLOTHES, PERFUME, MUSIC, CONFIRM FLIGHT, CHECK PERMITS.MARCH 2001 WITH SAYID IN MUHAMED TULEIB (KHARGA OASIS. EGYPT) 4 X MILK POWDER (SMALL) / 1X 23 LTR JERRYCAN / 1X 5 LTR JERRYCAN FOR SPIRITUS (EMPTY) / 2 BOXES COCOA AND BEEF CUBES / EMPTY PROVISION BAGS / 5 METER BLUE ROPE / QASR APRIL 2001 (DAKHLA OASIS, EGYPT) 2 SWEDISH JERRYCANS INFLATABLE / 3X 23 LTR JERRYCANS. CARABINER / IRON RING SADDLE / 5 METER THICK ROPE / THIN ROPE / 3 BUNDLES WHITE COTTON ROPE / ZIPPERS FOR BAGS / STRING FOR BAGS ABOUT 7 METER / 3 SADDLES / 2X 2 SADDLE CUSHIONS / 3 SADDLE BELTS / WHIP / LEATHER BELT / 8X OGAL / EQUIPMENT IN CANVAS BAG / 5 PLATES / 3 SPOONS / 5 MUGS / CAN OPENER / SERVING SPOON / HERBS / 2 BIG BOWLS / 1 SMALL / 2 TANGIA COOKING SETS / TEA CONSTRAINER / CONTAINER WASHING POWDER / 3X 1 LTR CONTAINER / BIG CONTAINER MILK POWDER / 2 SMALL FOR TANG POWDER / COTTON BAGS / RUBBER SLEEPING MAT / 4 TENT POLES / BAG WITH RUBBER BANDS / MEDICINES: 2X DEHYDRATION STUFF, ASPERINES, PLASTERS, TAPE, BANDAGE, MICROPUR STRIPS, OINTMENT BURNS, DESINFECTION, POLARPURE, TRACHITOL, COMPEED, SECOND SKIN SHEEP WOOL, LEUKOPLAST, SUNBLOCK LIPS, SUN CREAM FACTOR 30, PASTILLES THROAT, INJECTION NEEDLES CAMELS, CANDY THROAT, SCALPEL AND BLADES, SRL, SOAP / BLUE INSULATION BAG, TUPERWARE BOX / 5 LTR JERRYCANS SPIRITUS (HALF FULL) / CANVAS SHEET (BIG) / 2

*A woman explorer in
Egypt and Sudan*

The American University in Cairo Press

Arita Baaijens

Desert Songs

The
Camel
Is loaded to sing.
Look what poetry can do:
Untie the knot in the burlap sack
And lift the golden
Falcon
Out.

Hafiz

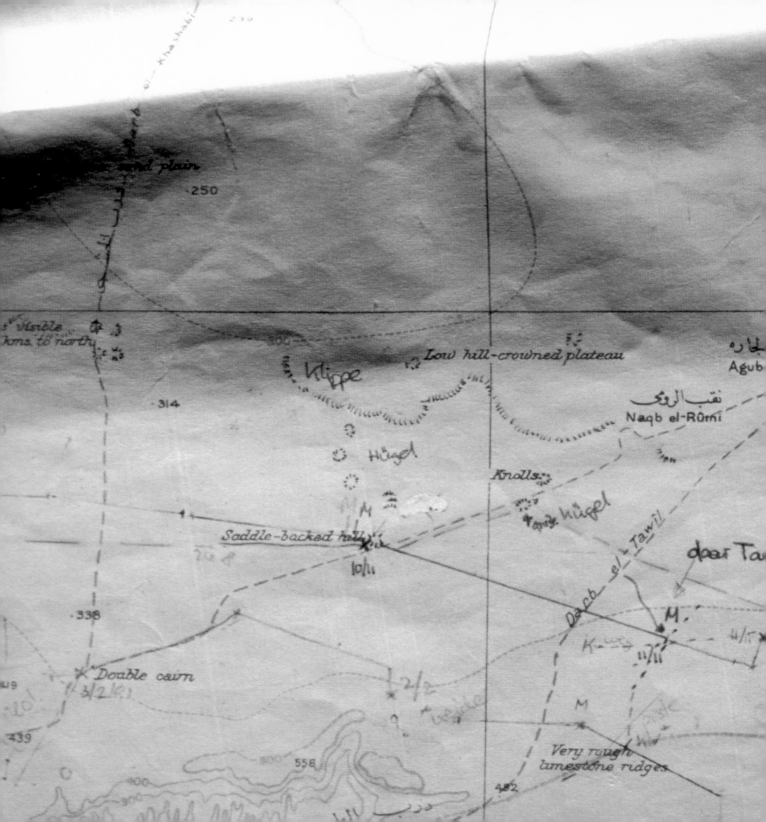

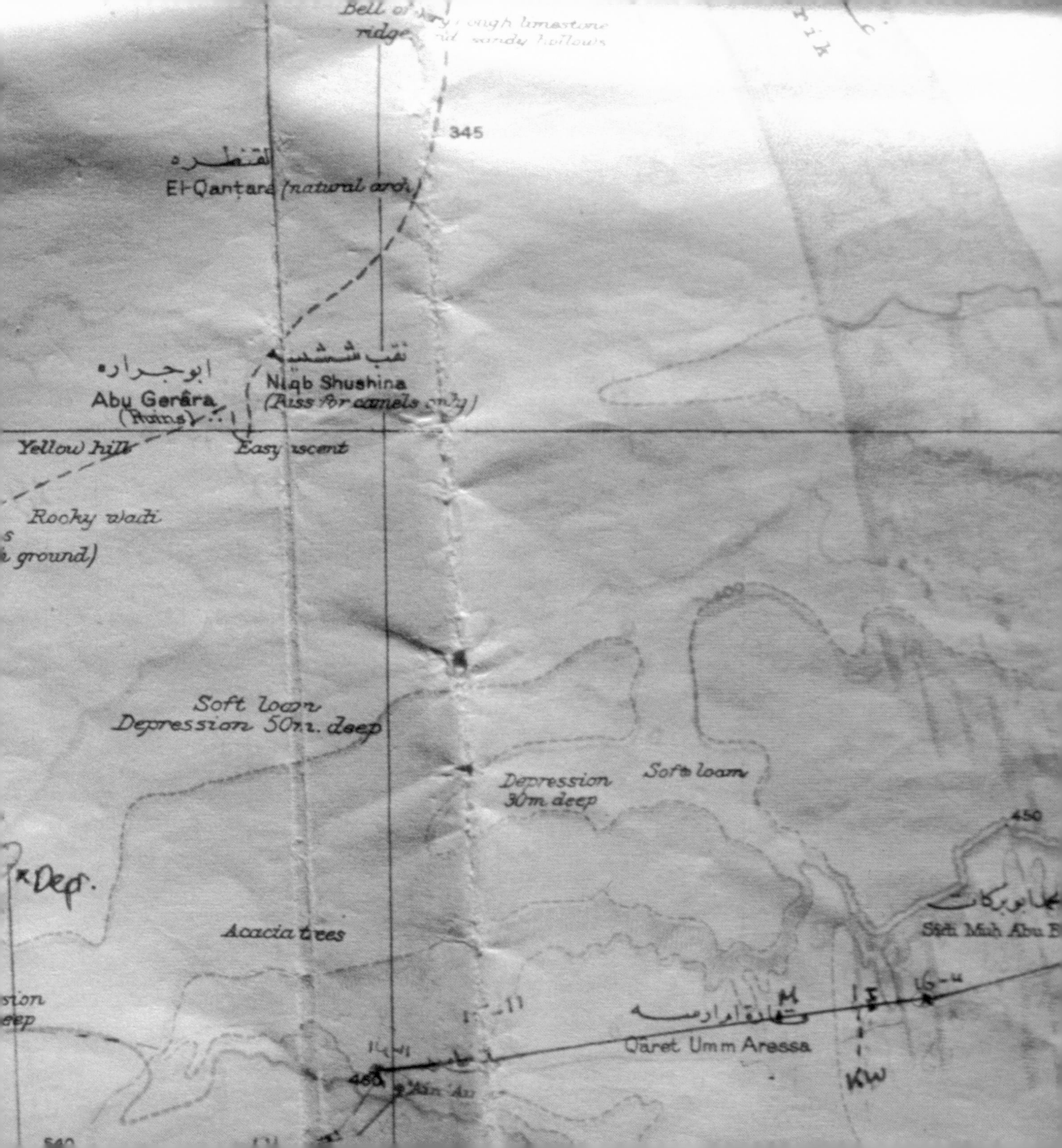

Bell of rough limestone
ridge and sandy hollows

345

القنطرة
El-Qantare (natural arch)

نقب ششينه

أبوجراره
Abu Gerâra
(Ruins)

Niqb Shushina
(Pass for camels only)

Yellow hill

Easy ascent

Rocky wadi

(d ground)

Soft loam
Depression 50m. deep

Depression
30m deep

Soft loam

450

×Dep.

Acacia trees

طحاحابوبركات
Sett. Mah Abu B

تخاندةامارسه
Qaret Umm Aressa

ion
eep

١٥-١١

١٦-٤

M

E

KW

460

Ain Au

540

I was alone.
For the first time
since I was born
it seemed to me
that my life
was my own
and that
I was responsible
for it.

Antoine de Saint-Exupéry

Sahara and Hassan enjoy a rest after a hard day's work. Soon the golden rays of the sun will set the dunes aflame, and later on the moon will bathe the earth in silvery light.

The
Desert
My
Home

For many years the desert had been a painting I gazed at with longing. My brief forays into the Sinai Desert did not count. What I was looking for was something larger and emptier, a continent, say, with vistas and horizons, freshly laundered skies, and abraded earth; a place I could disappear into for months without anyone noticing.

In the autumn of 1988 dream and reality came together. Bringing up the rear of a modest cortege of camels, I stepped out of the small Egyptian oasis known as Ain Tinin and straight through the frame of the painting, feeling very much like Alice in Wonderland. Still half dreaming, I followed the swishing camel tails, trudging across the powdery chalk sand into which I sank up to my ankles. It didn't bother me when – to put me to the test – my German guide marched for hours without a break. As I chewed on a piece of dry bread, my gaze was drawn to hills that resembled caterpillars and sickle-shaped sand dunes that seemed to embrace the desert.

It was a fairy-tale setting of blindingly white limestone rocks and sand dunes I loved to roll down. Occasionally I found the odd fossil or flintstone arrow, and I scoured the rock face in search of scratched symbols. I revelled in the desert wind and the spare, virgin landscape, still untouched by modern man because this desert was simply too large and too arid and too frightening.

I was serenely happy, but the same could not be said of the man who held my fate in his hands. I had spurned the advances of my desert guide, and I would have to leave the caravan. But how could I leave? I had embarked on this adventure with the inner conviction that it was going to change my life. That's why I stayed, hoping for a cease-fire, for peace of mind, so that I could enjoy the silence and the beauty of the desert undisturbed.

A month later I was so emotionally exhausted by all the arguments and slanging matches that I decided to return to civilization. I spent the last evening alone, so that I could take leave of the desert in peace. A full moon appeared from beneath the earth. Its majestic contours rose above the sand dunes as it glided regally skywards. The stars paled in comparison. Never had I seen the moon at such close quarters. Never had I imagined that its round face could be so large, and shine so compellingly.

I hardly slept that night, and not only because of the full moon. For a moment I toyed with the idea of trekking into the desert on my own. But the very thought frightened me half to death! Navigation was not my strong suit.

The next day I followed the camel tracks to the camp of my guide. He was enthusiastic about my somewhat vague plan to go it alone: 'That's exactly what I would have done in your place.' He gave me directions, a map, provisions and a camel. I could leave the following day. That was just a bit too fast for me, and maybe it was for that reason that he offered to follow me at a distance, in case I missed a water well. 'I'll manage just fine with a map and a compass', I said, with more bravura than I actually felt.

In fact, I very nearly missed the first water well, and I did miss the next one, after which my camel ran away and my watch stopped working, which meant I couldn't calculate the distance I had already travelled.

Peace and quiet were in short supply. Mabrouka missed the other camels and bellowed from dawn to dusk, while the desert presented its most hostile face. I saw the magnificence of the black-powdered chalk hills and the sand traces, but my stomach churned at the thought that somehow I would have to find my own way.

I asked myself why I was courting danger when there was no need to. No one expected anything of me, and it wasn't really much fun on my own. The only time I was actually happy was in the

The Roman temple of Deir el Hagar in Dakhla Oasis, Egypt, is dedicated to Seth, God of the oasis. One column of the sandstone temple bears the names of the members of Gerhard Rohlfs' expedition in 1873–74.

Meetings — While I seldom encountered a living soul in the Egyptian desert, there were more than enough meetings. Tracks left by narrow tyres, empty corned beef tins, and rusty fuel drums mark the route taken by the British Survey, who charted the area in the 20s and 30s. As I followed the deserted caravan roads, I fantasized about the travellers whose broken amphorae, jugs, and potsherds I found along the way. Gazing up at the graffiti on temple walls, I saw in my mind's eye the explorers who had left little beyond their signature; an old shoe, a piece of string, a pile of stones, a flint tool, or the bones of a traveller who died of thirst, finds that invariably gave rise to imaginary conversations with the people whose path I crossed so many centuries later.

It was in Sudan that I first met nomads. The shy and suspicious Beja who lived in the Red Sea Hills hardly ever showed themselves, but in other parts of the Sudanese desert I was seldom alone. When everyone else was asleep, I sought the company of the stars. Like faithful friends, they appeared in the sky at the appointed time and greeted me with their dazzling display.

evening, when Mabrouka sat quietly by my feet and the stars twinkled.

During the day, the sun forced me to keep walking. It was then that I had to make my decisions. But what difference did it make whether I headed for one hill or the other? It all seemed totally senseless. At home in Holland I got up when the alarm went off, I kept my appointments, exercised regularly several days a week, and on the weekends I went out. My whole life was governed by the expectations of others, and now that I had to fill the minutes and hours myself, I was at my wit's end.

The worst part was that I no longer knew who I was, now that there was no one around to laugh or cry with me, or take exception to something I said or did. The person I thought I was proved to be no more than the sum of what others thought of me. In this social vacuum, my old persona faded away. My identity disappeared – suddenly, without so much as a by-your-leave.

As I put one foot in front of the other, I wondered whose voice I was hearing in my head. Who or what was determining my actions? Where were my thoughts coming from and where were they going? My sense of space and time altered. Sometimes minutes went by during which my head was totally empty of thought: I was one with the sun and the camels, and everything was fine just the way it was. But as soon as a wisp of thought floated by, the clock started ticking again. Then I was conscious of the passing of time and cause and effect; conscious of a stone in my shoe, and the camel walking next to me. I saw the world as a magic trick and my mind as the magician who could make things disappear and reappear at will.

After a stay of three months in Egypt, I returned to Holland, to that austere polder landscape where human lives are governed by the minute hand of the clock. My desert journey had left me with

more questions than answers. And when I tried to pick up the thread of everyday life again, I knew that something had changed forever. My office job and my social life no longer held any attraction, and when I got home after work I was happy to sit for hours at a time, just staring in front of me. The walls receded and in my mind's eye I saw the spot where my soul was still wandering. I missed the horizon, the caress of the wind, fussing around with camels, and the languid rhythm of life.

In the desert I had toyed with the idea of giving up my job. The life of a nomad had appealed to me, but now I realized that here in Holland I was encapsulated, protected. As an adventurer, I would be placing myself outside society. Which is all well and good when you're young, but how would I cope as I got older? What would become of me if I gave up everything? The longer I thought about it, the more unreal the plan seemed.

But a year later, after my second desert journey, all doubts disappeared. During a stay of several months, surrounded by sand and rocks, I discovered that the longing for solitude and a life on the edge had not been an illusion. Heat, cold, thirst, discomfort, and exhaustion did not bother me, and giving up my resistance to things I had no power to change had a beneficial effect on my spirit. My life now centred solely on camels and on finding water. The world beyond simply did not exist. It was glorious to walk for hours on end, occasionally looking back to check on the camels. As they plodded on, the simple bobbing of their heads encouraged me. Thoughts came but quickly evaporated. More often, I thought about nothing at all and was happier than I had ever thought possible. What difference did it make that I still could not put into words what drove me to the desert? A longing cannot always be explained, but it is still there, like the sun, the moon and the stars. The anxious voices that had plagued me when I was in Holland gradually fell silent. I saw myself as an elderly lady,

After our arrest in the desert a soldier accompanied the caravan from Abu Simbel to Kharga oasis.

Camels

— Camels are the bearers of my dreams. A throbbing engine is no substitute for the gentle shuffle of camel feet. Watching the landscape streak by from behind a dusty windscreen is not the same as registering each metre you traverse, on foot or on the gently swaying back of a camel. In this relaxed tempo, you are conscious of each and every change: you feel the wind, submit to heat and cold, and undergo the languid passage of time.

For me, a desert without camels is unthinkable. I love their grumpiness, the pungent smell of their urine, and the eternal smile that hovers around their fleshy lips. Even their typical haughty look and their vociferous protestations when I saddle them have become dear to me.

There are no more beautiful creatures on earth than camels, except of course baby camels. And I'm not the only one who holds this view. In countless poems, nomads have celebrated the exceptional qualities of this magnificent animal. Camel dung provides fuel, the women weave sturdy tents from camel's hair, their urine is a sure cure for head lice, and camel's milk is not only nourishing, but also full of vitamin C. As a Bedouin poet once declaimed: the camel is worth more than money can buy.

with a lovely home, a car in the garage, and a healthy bank balance. While money and security are not unimportant, the crucial question was: From my vantage point in the lap of luxury, how would I look back on a life that had not been fully lived?

Having decided to quit my job, I felt a tremendous sense of relief. I was free as I had never been before, simply because I had nothing more to lose. Never again would I allow myself to be fenced in by convention and false certainties. From now on, I would rely on the voice of my heart.

It is in the desert that Nature shows us its most uncompromising face. The magnificent play of shadows, the comforting flood of light, and the gold glow of the sand are there, of course, but only when the sun is low on the horizon. During the hours in between, the sunlight is hard and unflattering, and it is then that the desert reveals its cruel side: equally beautiful, but disquieting.

The desert kills where it can, and the instinct for survival infuses us with courage and vitality. Face to face with danger, the blood is fired up, the eye becomes keener, and blunted senses come to life again. It is no longer possible to rely on routine, and there is no time to worry about futilities. To survive in the desert, you must be prepared to give up everything, and this is a trial of strength which involves facing up to hard facts. How strong are you when there's no back-up? Can you handle fear and panic, or do the demons in the furthest reaches of your mind get the upper hand? Where do your limits lie? This is precisely what I intended to find out on my third desert journey, in the winter of 1990, the year I quit my job. There was a good chance that the 400-kilometre trek across the waterless desert between the oases of Farafra and Kharga would end in disaster. And yet I was not weary of life when I made my decision. On the contrary.

Facing up to the challenge of death was a way of overcoming my fear of life. Somewhere deep inside I knew that if this journey was successful, I would never be afraid of anything again.

'November 10, 1990. The caravan threads its way through the hills. Perfunctorily I record my course changes, noting how many minutes I've walked in a certain direction. After weeks of plodding, I no longer trust my notes. The map is a meaningless scrap of paper, and terms like open sand plain and rough limestone plateau say nothing about the moonless landscape around me. The desert where I felt so much at home for all those years now offers no solace. It wrings from me sweat and blood. My head is empty, and my body, too. Gatifa regularly collapses and the last link with reality seems to have disappeared. I don't think about yesterday or tomorrow. Nothing exists except the here and now.'

When I wrote these words in my diary, the point of no return was already behind me. Standing on the ragged edge of a limestone plateau with two exhausted camels, I had looked down to see an oasis. I could have gone back then, but I turned around and headed for the sand dunes, dragging the camels grimly behind me, down one dune and up the next.

Gatifa was close to exhaustion, and I was in pretty bad shape myself. But there could be no question of giving up. My fate was bound up with this journey: I could not face a life without certainty or security until I knew how strong I was. Giving up now would endanger my future. It would also be tantamount to moral suicide.

Some people may find it hard to believe that a person is willing to die for an idea. And yet there was considerable truth in my reasoning, as witness all those myths and legends about heroes who voluntarily undertake a perilous quest with no regard for their own safety.

The journey into uncertainty symbolizes

It was love at first sight when I met the Polish archaeologist Krzysztof Pluskota in Old Dongola in Sudan. Krzysztof introduced me to the Beja, and together we explored their mountainous homeland in eastern Sudan.

Love — *Passion and single-mindedness are part of life in the desert. The threat of death and the instinct for survival call up strong emotions, and amid the desolation of sand and rock, strange things can happen. You can be gripped by madness or rapture, love or hate. But there is no room for that grey middle ground, where lukewarm hearts thrive. In the city feelings can be kept under control, but the desert is exacting: it demands submission and will not tolerate hidden agendas. It's all or nothing at all.*

Today I see love as a kind of salto mortale without a safety net. If you are not prepared to fall to your death, you will never know ecstasy.

But love isn't only about deep emotions. It also involves dedication, giving without expecting anything in return. In the words of the Persian mystic Hafiz, 'Even after all this time, the sun never says to the earth: "you owe me." A love like that lights up the whole sky.'

the transition to adulthood, a rite of passage which no longer arouses much interest in the Western world. On the surface, at least, for primeval urges are universal and the veneer of civilization thin.

During that journey I laid to rest panic, fear of death, and my own madness. Those experiences changed me forever. The moments of happiness also had a decisive influence on the rest of my life. Pure bliss was occasioned by such seemingly unimportant things as the rising and setting of the sun, a miracle I never got used to. Or a cool breeze that dried the perspiration on my forehead, the sight of dreamy camels just outside my night camp, the horseshoe of saddle bags that formed my 'house' wherever I set up camp. So little was needed to evoke a deep sense of contentment. At night I sometimes crawled out of my sleeping bag and walked across the sand, shivering with cold, but blissfully happy because I was one with the glittering stars, the immeasurable space around me, and the cool sand underneath my feet. The emptiness, the silence, the surrender to what there is, the awareness that I am everything and nothing: at moments like this insights came to me that were gone again a minute later. But they had left their mark, for my heart overflowed and my head seemed about to explode.

It is amazing how quickly one becomes accustomed to a new life. I was now a bird of passage who became impatient as soon as the leaves began to turn, heralding the arrival of autumn. When at night the winter constellation of Orion wafted across the Amsterdam sky like an oversized butterfly, I began counting the days and looking forward to my reunion with the camels. Every winter I explored a different white spot on the map, searching for old, forgotten caravan routes, rock engravings, and temple ruins. Not only were these explorations exciting, they also served to structure the months I spent in the desert.

I was on my way before daybreak, and I greeted the sun with one eye on the map and compass. I seldom spent two nights in the same place, the journey is more important than the arrival. The caravan covered a distance of some forty kilometres a day, and loading and unloading involved lifting hundreds of kilos. On arrival, I tended to the camels, set up camp, lugged heavy water barrels and feed bags, and slept under the stars. After calculating the route I'd travelled that day, I updated my diary and was dead to the world by seven o'clock.

I do not want to romanticize my life in the desert. It is a harsh existence with at least as many lows as highs. There is no enjoyment involved in battling sandstorms for days or even weeks at a time, discovering that the camels have run off, or listening to the plaintive bellowing of animals that are hungry or thirsty. I do not feel particularly brave standing on the edge of a cliff face that I know I must descend, even though I'm not sure how and the camels are rearing in terror and crapping all over everything. And yet it is infinitely more satisfying to take on the elements than to join the frantic rat race to get ahead in your chosen profession.

The outside world I was so eager to escape from caught up with me a few years later. Deep wells and ribbons of asphalt in the furthest reaches of the Egyptian desert were the forerunners of large-scale agricultural projects. Even more far-reaching was the arrival of the GPS, a satellite navigation system that turned the desert into a playground for motorized tourism. Naturally, I know that the desert is not mine alone. And yet I cursed them, those newcomers who treat the desert as if it's disposable, something that provides a brief moment of enjoyment and is then discarded. The untouched landscape and the old caravan routes are now covered by a network of deep car tracks, incurable open wounds, above which hang the lingering overtones of gasoline and sun-tan oil.

Ain Amur. This domestic scene showing a woman herding ducks indicates that people once lived in this remote spot halfway up a cliff in the middle of the Egyptian desert.

Discoveries — *The desert is an open-air museum without the 'Please do not touch' signs. Objects from different eras lie companionably next to one another, like the scattered pages of an old history book. Celts and scrapers and bracelets from prehistoric times alongside Roman jugs and pre-war petrol cans. In the northeast of Sudan I once found myself in the deserted mountain shaft of a gold mine dating back to the ancient Egyptian empire. Those same mountains were home to mysterious prehistoric graves, huge round structures made of bits and pieces of stone. In the Tagabo Hills in Darfur, I saw the ruins of mountain cities. No one knew who had lived there or when they were built.*

Roman tollhouses, temples, forts and underground water systems. Old graves with mummies wrapped in linen. Hieroglyphs in rocks. The diorite mine of the pharaoh Chephren. Each find is a journey back in time, along the tattered umbilical cord linking us to the past, to people who knew joy and pain, prosperity and misfortune. The wheel of life and death continues to turn and spares no one. I leave these discoveries intact, to ensure that the history behind them is not lost. One day I shall die too, and who would know the story behind the jugs and shards on my windowsill?

The desecration of everything I held dear drove me to Sudan, where war and violence keep tourists at bay. In the largest country in Africa, I found a home among nomads who tend camels: proud, freedom-loving men and women whose shrewd gaze is always on the horizon.

The transition from an uninhabited to an inhabited desert was significant. I had to get used to the invisible eyes that followed my every move, and the dangers that lurked all around me. Raids and shootings were an everyday occurrence in Sudan, and it was not always safe for me to travel on my own. Least of all in the state of Darfur, in the far west of Sudan. Even before the war began in 2003, the area was made unsafe by the presence of bandits, who first emptied their guns and then demanded the spoils. In North Kordofan a single armed escort had been sufficient, but in Darfur I was accompanied by two bodyguards and the elderly desert guide Yussuf Gamaa, who also served as a chaperone. The men were extremely courteous, but it was clear that they did not take my desert experience or navigational skills very seriously, and my sense of curiosity puzzled them. In fact, the idea of someone travelling through such territory purely out of curiosity is incomprehensible to a nomad whose life hangs permanently by a thread. My companions soon forgot why they had been hired, and while I was interested in rock carvings, the ruins of old cities, and a salt lake in the midst of a sand sea, they couldn't wait to leave Darfur behind them. I had to fight for each new destination, and as the weeks passed I found myself losing my temper more and more often, something which the Sudanese regard as a serious transgression. In other areas, too, the cultural differences were considerable. Where the nomads had to contend with severe limitations in the area of food, water, health care, education and employment, I lived in a land of plenty, and was accustomed to thinking ahead in order to preclude risks.

But there was no way of avoiding the dangers inherent in life in Sudan. There was no insurance policy that covered bombs, lack of rain, epidemics, and military coups. In a crisis you turned to family or to Allah. There were no other options.

Mentally, my fellow travellers and I weren't even on the same planet, but I did feel a genuine kinship with my desert guide. It was as if I was closer to a man like Yussuf, who had known famines and once lost his whole camel herd during a drought, than to the upwardly mobile young people in my own country. And as far as danger is concerned, the chances of being caught up in a gun battle were no greater than the likelihood of being involved in a traffic accident in Amsterdam.

That's how I felt about Darfur when the rule of law and conflict mediation were still functioning. It was only when war broke out, shortly after my last journey, that I realized just how much was going on beneath the surface.

Travelling through Sudan, I sometimes longed for the solitude of the Egyptian desert. And yet back in Egypt, I missed the camaraderie, talking around the fire, and the chance meetings with nomads. But regardless of whether I was in Sudan or Egypt, more and more my thoughts were returning to those early years in the desert. The intensity of life, the obsession, that all-or-nothing feeling, had disappeared for good. I realized that I no longer travelled because I had to, but out of habit. It was a painful discovery. And yet the loss of my obsession marked a new beginning. The desert had finished with me. It was time to move on. In the meantime, I have spread my wings and embraced other regions. But the decision to take leave of the desert for good is apparently one I cannot take.

Desert Songs is a journey through time: an ode to my camels and to the desert, which for twenty years has been my home.

I am an old man.
Although I have had
many desires in life,
I never married
because I could not leave
my beloved camels.

Somali poem

Camels

Mabrouka One
Mabrouka Two
Sahara
Naxla
Arabella
Mabrouka Three
Hassan
Sahara
Rashid
Atbara
Amur

Wario
Gatifa
Wolfje
Muskaat
Sjachatour
Hassan jr
Hiluxi
Ashan
Hidashar
Morena
Amira

It was love at first sight with Mabrouka, the female camel who accompanied me on that first desert adventure twenty years ago. She was beautiful, with her curly coat, slender legs, graceful neck, and magnificent head. Her frightened eyes shone when we led her out of the Egyptian oasis of Farafra.

Mabrouka had never been alone. She missed the herd and bellowed with homesickness. Often she threw the loads off by bucking. I sympathized with this reluctant beauty. We were both newcomers in the caravan and I was still getting used to the situation myself. During the stops, the high-handed and unpredictable behaviour of the caravan leader drove me to take refuge with Mabrouka, who hadn't connected either. Sahara and Arabella, the other female camels, regarded her as an intruder and the standoffish male, Hassan, remained aloof.

Mabrouka and I slowly grew in our roles. During later solo trips, she walked at the front of my caravan, calm and self-assured. Her extensive repertoire of noises cheered me up on tiring day marches. When I climbed a hill to reconnoitre the route, she waited patiently at the bottom. Sometimes she burrowed her soft muzzle in my neck when she wanted to stop for a break, and in the evenings her head rested in my lap. Mabrouka's familiar camel silhouette at the foot of my desert bed was enough to banish sombre thoughts and feelings of loneliness.

Mabrouka died as the result of a snakebite, and at markets I searched for a reincarnation of my favourite camel. And I found Mabrouka Two and Mabrouka Three. They, too, had a curly coat and a pretty face, and they conversed with me. But my heart was not fooled. No other camel has ever been able to take the place of the real Mabrouka.

Camels do not like descents. Going downhill with stretched legs involves a jolting movement which a camel finds unpleasant with a full load on its back.

I wrote my first book in an uninhabited Egyptian oasis called Labakha. The camels grazed near the camp and often came by in search of a snack.

Adolescent camels

Character—Not all camels are the same, I realized, as I stood at the edge of a 300-metre-high limestone plateau. A steep sand slide made it possible to descend, but the lead camel was afraid of heights. It was not until the others had reached the bottom that separation anxiety got the better of her fear of heights, and she slid down the slope.

This was not the first time I was caught unawares by the peculiarities of camels. One had a fear of climbing. Another refused to cross bridges. Sometimes my camels would take fright at a rock in the sand dunes. But there are spunky camels, too, born leaders with a cold-blooded streak. Unfortunately, it's only after the deal is done that you find out whether the new acquisition is brave or timorous, or lazy, or just plain full of mischief.

On my solo journeys I much prefer female camels or nagas. They're less strong than a male camel, but they're friendly and don't go around attacking people the way a dakkar does, plagued as he is by male hormones.

Camels do not readily bond with human beings, but they do remember their smell and whether they were treated well or badly by a particular individual. A mistreated dakkar will patiently await his chance. Then he will toss his tormenter out of the saddle or chase after him, throw him to the ground and crush him to death.

Happily, there are also affectionate camels. Little Rashid followed me around like an orphaned chick when his mother was cross with him, and at night his head rested on the saddlebag next to my desert bed. Sahara regularly joined me beside the campfire. Bousie sprawled on her side when I petted her.

Camels come in different shapes and sizes, but there's not one that doesn't have a mind of his own.

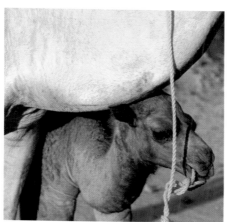

Young camels—There is nothing that compares with being awakened by the bawling of young camels. The crying of a human baby is annoying, but the plaintive wails of baby camels thirsting for milk is melodious. I don't even mind it when they muck about in camp, the youngsters are allowed to race around, knock over cooking pots, and even jump on me in the middle of the night.

Where camels are concerned, I'm never too tired, whether it means observing them, training them, or playing games with them. Baby camels are quick learners. Only days old, they respond to their name, and after a brief course of training, they will sit on command. They are also surprisingly tough. When they were only a week old, Muskaat and Hassan were doing twenty kilometres a day. Ashan was born around the same time, in the middle of the desert. I stuffed the long-legged baby into a bag filled with straw and hung it on a saddle. The mother didn't seem at all surprised to see that the head of her newborn calf was suddenly two metres higher.

During breaks the baby camels occasionally got hold of the wrong udder. When a short-tempered auntie nipped them, they'd race into the desert, bellowing at the top of their lungs, and leave me to deal with their indignant mothers.

Wario and Wolfje came into the world in the Red Sea Hills of Sudan. I hated the thought of having to sell the babies and their mothers at the end of the journey, but my companion found a reliable buyer. Beja sheikh Issa Ba'adeen treated his camels like much-loved pets, and promised not to sell them. The sheikh kept his word. A Sudanese aid worker who visited the area two years later reported that Wolfje and Wario were thriving.

Descent—Mabrouka Two panics. Her pack saddle has shifted and the heavy jerry cans are pressing against her neck. I have to leave the bags behind and come back later to drag them down the slope.

33

The broad, flat foot of
a camel resembles a tyre
filled with fat. It is
perfect for travelling on
sand, but less suitable
for stony deserts and
slippery surfaces. The
foot is supported on the
inside by a soft, fatty
pad.

Camels feeding in green
pastures lose 6 or 7
litres of water a day
through their faeces.
Dry food results in a
loss of 1.3 litres. They
produce one-half to 9
litres of urine per day,
depending on the type
of food and the avail-
ability of water.

Nose tissue absorbs
water from exhaled air.
The blood in the cool-
ing system of the nose
passages provides some
respite for nose, eyes
and brain. The camel's
hairy but sensitive
upper lip is split and
extensible.

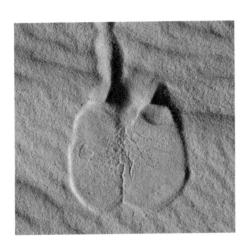
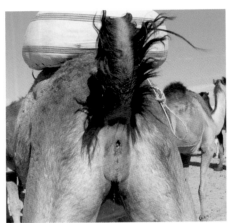

The ship of the desert—

Camels are so perfectly suited to their surroundings that no engineer could possibly improve on the basic model. The hump and the woolly hair block the rays of the sun. When they sit down, the cushions of calloused skin on their knees and chest protect them against the burning desert sand. Their flat, leathery foot soles are the camel's own equivalent of snowshoes. Heavy lashes and hairy ears keep the sand out.

The camel is the only mammal with oval-shaped blood cells. When its body cells absorb fluid from the plasma, making the blood more viscous, these oval blood cells still glide through the animal's veins, ensuring that organs and brain continue to function. The 'ship of the desert' can withstand a rise in body temperature of 7 degrees Celsius, which makes sweating all but unnecessary. The nose filters fluid out of each breath exhaled, and when water intake is insufficient, the animal's dung becomes drier and the volume of urine decreases.

Over a longer period, fluid loss can cause a camel to lose up to a quarter of its body weight. But when it is finally able to slake its thirst, it can put away a hundred litres of water in a matter of minutes. The head of an adult camel is normally at a height of two and a half metres, where in summer it is some 30 degrees cooler than on the ground. The long neck serves as both periscope and ladder: trees and bushes are visible from a distance, and higher branches disappear effortlessly into the wide-open maw.

The camel may be a biological miracle, but its comical appearance brings it no joy. Legend has it that on the day of Creation the camel looked at its image in a pool of water and was so mortified that it fled into the desert.

Before starting out on a journey, I give my camels salt, which increases water intake and improves metabolism.

Camels will keep going until they collapse. Having succumbed to fatigue, they seldom manage to get back on their feet.

Camels love dry food. Wherever they are, they'll come running when they hear the rattle of a grain bucket.

Food—Camels and barren sand dunes go together, at least in photo books. In actual fact, however, camels much prefer bushes and grass to sand. Given the opportunity, they would eat all day, and a free-grazing camel can put away 10 to 20 kilos of green food a day. Regardless of whether the vegetation is rich or poor, a camel will stay on the move while it feeds and can easily cover 20 kilometres a day. Luckily, hobbled camels don't get that far, but even a hobbled run-away spells trouble for a poor tracker like me.

In a barren environment, pack camels carry lunch and dinner on their back. The daily requirement of a hard-working camel is about 5 kilos of dorra, or sorghum. On long journeys my female camels, who carry my water and food supplies, have to survive on half the required amount. Small wonder that humps soon shrink and ribs begin to protrude accusingly. And yet a large hump full of fat does not necessarily increase the animals' chances of survival. A scrawny, humpless desert camel who is used to arid conditions tolerates a shortage of food and water much better than a meaty camel that has fed on rich pastures. Camels, like people, must get used to long working hours and little food and water. Which is why I train my camels so rigorously before the start of a journey.

The water requirement of a camel will depend on its age, the thickness of its coat, the workload, and the ambient temperature. A trained pack camel on dry feed can go an average of two weeks without water at temperatures of up to 35 degrees.

After a working stint of several weeks, my camels are ready for a rest. Then we settle down on pasture land or get some rest and relaxation in an oasis.

Camp Bagawat—*The tombs of Bagawat in Kharga Oasis, Egypt, date from the fourth century. I had come here to consult a veterinarian for Morena, who had a saddle wound. For the rest of the journey my other two camels had to carry her load as well.*

Loading—Nomads need no more than a travelling blanket, a handful of dates, and a full water sack. But I am a bag lady who lugs along an average of eighteen saddlebags, filled with jerry cans, sorghum, tools, and provisions. The cameras, lenses, and films are wrapped in reinforced bags. A large saddlebag is reserved for clothes, medicine, a sleeping bag and a sleeping mat. I also take along piles of maps, and gifts for people I meet on the way.

Nomads shake their heads in disbelief at the 'needs' of the Western traveller. But I grew up in the city and, moreover, I lack

their deep-rooted faith in God. But I do wear amulets, the neatly folded aphorisms in small leather pouches guaranteed to protect me against scorpions, thieves, and stray bullets.

Loading a camel is an exact science, one which starts with the correct placement of the saddle. The saddle belt has to fit tightly around the belly, to ensure that the saddle doesn't shift. Cushions on the inside of a wooden saddle prevent blisters. The load on the right and the left side must be in balance. Heavy feed bags and water bags hang underneath, with the lighter bags on top. A rope fastened

around the whole pile keeps things from flapping and prevents dangerous shifting.

The lead camel carries the camera case. The things I need during the day hang on the front pommel for easy access: the shoulder bag with maps, my diary, sunscreen, ropes, and candy. On top are the binoculars and a water bottle. The final item is the whip.

When everything's in place, I peer out over the sand. Has anything been left behind? After going through my checklist, I tie the camels to each other and finally set the caravan in motion.

Pack saddles are hard to come by in Egypt, but in Sudan there is a wide selection. For repairs, I use thin plastic rope. The pads are made from large, loosely woven plastic bags, stuffed with sturdy grass.

Nomads repair the worn soles of their camels' feet with a round piece of leather, which they sew onto the foot with a leather lace. The operation is painless if the sole hasn't become too thin.

A rope and a piece of wood are all it takes to make an ogal or knee hobble.

Equipment—In the desert I developed a passion for string and rope. Thick or thin, soft or fibrous, made of leather, cotton or plastic. My nylon line, good for repairing saddle bags, comes from Holland. At markets in Egypt and Sudan I keep an eagle eye out for cotton that's guaranteed to break when subjected to a certain strain. If I find just the right kind of plastic-coated wire I need to put together a camel saddle, I buy everything they have in stock. I always order heavy rope by the roll. A slightly thicker version is just right for ogals, or knee-hobbles. Strong but soft rope is ideal for joining the head and tail of a protesting camel when festering wounds have to be cleansed. And I use narrow leather thongs to fasten a piece of leather around the worn sole of a camel's foot.

Far from civilization, my pottering skills come to the fore: in the desert I am vet, midwife, and car mechanic all rolled into one. Broken saddles are mended using wooden pegs, lengths of rope, a couple of spoons and a knife. I repair torn camel soles, dress stinking wounds, administer injections, and in time to the rhythm of the contractions, I pull baby camels into the world by their soft little feet.

Of course, I'm no match for the nomads when it comes to desert know-how and the care and treatment of camels. Those survival experts taught me that a bent whip will straighten itself out when buried in wet sand, a drinking trough is a hole in the sand lined with a piece of canvas, and a handful of salt cures eye infections. Rolling a stick over the camel's neck will remedy an obstructed gullet.

In the desert, ingenuity is the hallmark of a master. The true professional is conspicuous not for his tools, but for the lack of them.

Camels at sunset—Free-grazing camels rest after sunset, but these hungry animals grazed all night in the Wadi Millik, in Sudan. The camels were being taken to Egypt and had not eaten for days when they arrived in the wadi.

Qasr Dakhla, Dakhla Oasis, Egypt

Good quality. Water level very low.
The water wells in the gardens in Qasr Dakhla
are difficult to access. Luckily, wells have been
drilled in the surrounding hills to irrigate the
land. The artesian water level in Dakhla oasis
is dropping at an alarming rate due to the high
consumption of water.

Ain Serru, White Desert, Egypt

Roman hot spring. Warm water wells up.
The sweet water spring atop a mound of its
debris dates back to Roman times. Before
tourists took over the White Desert this spot
was a quiet paradise. I used to bathe in the
small pool with the beautiful view.

Ain Farah, North Darfur, Sudan

Sweet water. Animal dung and urine.
*The water pool in a sandstone canyon is an
important watering place for the Tunjur
people. Nearby is a garden with lemon trees
The ruins of an ancient fortress and a mosque
are situated on top of the granite mountain
adjacent to the pool.*

Malha crater, North Darfur, Sudan

Contaminated water. Not good for drinking.
The Malha crater is 7000 years old. Sweet water is released through cracks in the bottom of the lake. The water is contaminated with animal urine and dung. Anaerobe bacteria colour the syrupy water bright green and purple. Camels and cattle drink from wells around the lake.

Merga lake, Nukheila Oasis, North Darfur, Sudan

Salt. Sweet water in dunes around the lake.
For years I dreamt about visiting Nukheila oasis, the lake and the palm trees in the surrounding sand dunes. The place is remote and difficult to reach. When I visited the oasis in the year 2000 I shed tears of joy. I couldn't swim in the lake, my desert guide warned me. The water monster would eat me.

No one in The Hague understood what possessed Alexandrine to continue the journey after losing her mother and her aunt. In that faraway land the young heiress was surrounded by people who had an eye on her money. Members of her staff died of malaria, bearers deserted, and there was the constant threat of raids. In the past, her mother and her aunt had taken a great deal of the work of organizing an expedition off her hands. Now Alexandrine Tinne faced this gigantic task alone.

I was among those who wondered what had motivated Alexandrine to seek out the hardships and dangers of Africa.

'If you look at the charts, you'll see that in the southwest, in the direction of the equator, there is a large space without a name. That's where we want to go. How far we will get I do not know.' In a letter written in 1863, Alexandrine Tinne reports that she and her mother — together with five sailing boats, sixty armed soldiers, donkeys, camels, a horse, hunters, carpenters and interpreters — were planning to sail up the White Nile with no more ambitious aim than to see how far they could get. This may sound somewhat improbable at a time when explorers were vying with one another to be the first to reach the sources of the Nile. But apparently Alexandrine was not interested in fame and recognition: as a wealthy and pampered young woman, she didn't have to prove anything to anyone.

There in the unknown heart of Africa she must have seen and heard and experienced exceptional things, but she never made her findings public. Was Alexandrine simply a tourist at heart, someone who delighted in tramping through boggy swamps, sweltering jungles, and barren deserts? In any case, she did not keep a diary, nor did she publish her findings public in scientific journals, and her letters were often full of trivialities.

She has been described as a feather-

Alexandrine Tinne was an enthusiastic photographer.
Above: The spouses of the crew of her sailing vessel De Meeuw. The crew members accompanied Alexandrine into the desert.
Below: Algiers 1867. The crew of De Meeuw, in Bedouin dress.

brain, albeit a wealthy featherbrain. It was said that the richest heiress in Holland threw her money around, and drove up the price of provisions, pack animals, and soldiers because she never haggled, much to the annoyance of less well-off Africa travellers, such as Samuel Baker (1821–1892).

And yet Alexandrine was by no means stupid. Her famous contemporary Dr. Livingstone was full of praise for this courageous and determined young woman, who surmounted enormous difficulties. Alexandrine also spoke six languages and had an inquiring mind. For example, she was one of the first in Holland to explore the possibilities of photography, a new phenomenon which required infinite patience and considerable technical skill. In The Hague, the young heiress even had a small coach fitted out as a darkroom, and on her travels she took along heavy cameras, glass plates, and chemicals.

The last photos of Alexandrine Tinne were taken in Libya, where she was making preparations for a trip across the Sahara. After several weeks, the expedition was stranded in the vicinity of Murzuk, where she was murdered by Tuareg who were after her well-filled strongboxes. Neither the culprits nor Alexandrine's last resting place were ever found.

It is unfortunate that Alexandrine Tinne was not able to complete her journey from Tripoli to Lake Chad, Darfur and Khartoum, for had she done so, the heiress who came to such a tragic end would truly have made history. All criticism would have been silenced by the fact that she — a woman — was the first explorer to cross the Sahara.

Rosita Forbes
1893–1967

Rosita Forbes travelled to the Libyan oasis of Kufra, disguised as a Muslim woman. She changed her name to Khadija, posing as the daughter of an Egyptian merchant and a Circassian woman, a slave from the harem of a sultan in Tunis.

It was sometime in the mid-nineties that I first heard of the flamboyant British writer and journalist Rosita Forbes. In *The Lost Oases*, by the Egyptian diplomat and explorer Hassanein Bey, she was named as the companion with whom he succeeded in reaching Kufra, centre of the strict Islamic Senussi Brotherhood, located in a mysterious oasis in a hidden corner of Libya. These sketchy details piqued my curiosity. Why had I never heard of this plucky lady before and why did her account of the journey, *Secret of the Sahara: Kufara*, not appear in the bibliographies of desert literature? I delved into archives and library sources in search of answers.

The Englishwoman Rosita Forbes, born into the landed gentry, was seventeen when she followed her husband Colonel Forbes to India and Australia. The marriage failed, but Rosita Forbes continued on her way, travelling alone through Africa, Asia, and the Middle East. After the First World War this traveller and engaged journalist turned up in Cairo when it was swarming with spies and intriguers. There she formed contacts which culminated in the desert journey that would make her famous in her day.

The Kufra adventure began in December 1920, when Rosita Forbes and the Egyptian diplomat Hassanein Bey left the northern coast of Libya with a small camel caravan, a desert guide, and several camel men. At night the crew slept under the stars while the handsome Hassanein shared a tent with the temperamental Forbes. The British gossip columns were soon regaling readers with details of the idiosyncratic behaviour of 'the woman whose lipstick never smudged', even in

The journey to Kufra was dangerous. Strangers were not welcome in these parts, and the threat of an assassination attempt hung over the caravan like an ominous shadow. Plans to kill Forbes and Hassanein were discovered in time and thwarted.

the middle of the desert. Even more damaging to her reputation were the rumours doing the rounds in Hassanein Bey's own circles. His influential friends were shocked that in her book about the journey to Kufra Rosita Forbes made it appear that she had taken the initiative for this daring expedition. 'Hassanein Bey assured me that he came for a rest cure,' wrote Forbes, sketching the Egyptian – an Oxford graduate – as a dapper scatterbrain. 'I had to superintend the packing lest he ignore the claims of malted milk tablets, towels and woollen underclothing in favour of delicately striped shirts and a lavender and silver dressing-gown!'

The British establishment in Cairo was not amused. Hassanein Bey belonged to the old boys' network and Rosita Forbes had insulted all of them with her banter. Why had she ridiculed her companion? Perhaps she was a woman disappointed in love. Or perhaps it was ambition that made her claim the fame. Whatever the reason, Rosita Forbes downplayed Hassanein Bey's contribution to their success and the diplomat could not defend himself, since a scandal would jeopardize his career.

Two years after their heroic journey, Hassanein Bey set out to explore the vast unknown desert which lay beyond Kufra. And this time he made sure no-body could rob him of his glory: his only companions were illiterate desert men.

While Rosita Forbes' attempt to grab the glory is indefensible, it does not detract from her physical and mental accomplishments. She made a considerable contribution to the success of the enterprise. In preparation, she learned Arabic and studied the Koran, and also became proficient in navigation, poring over maps and old travel accounts. It was Rosita who purchased the provisions and visited high-placed individuals in order to acquire the necessary travel documents. She obtained a letter of introduction to Mohammad Idris, the emir of the Senussi.

Photos taken by Rosita Forbes with a small Kodak camera.
Above: December 1920. The caravan is heading for Kufra, an oasis in a far corner of Libya.
Below: In early January of 1921 the party arrives in Kufra, exhausted and half-dead from thirst.

It was thanks to that letter, together with Hassanein Bey's connections, that the two Saharan explorers were given permission to travel to Kufra. But the suspicious Senussi still made several attempts to murder the unwanted travellers. Although Rosita Forbes later made light of the dangers, the hunger and thirst, and the sand storms which plagued them during the thousand-kilometre journey through no-man's land, they were very close to death on several occasions. The return trip was equally laborious. When Hassanein Bey had a fall and broke his collarbone, Rosita Forbes travelled on ahead to get help. While the diplomat was recovering from his injuries, she enjoyed to the hilt the receptions held in her honour in Cairo. While she may have exaggerated her role as the leader of the expedition during those dinners and receptions, should we really fault this female explorer for her self-importance? It is usually the men who try to downplay the role of women in history. Just this once, it was the other way around.

Douglas Newbold
1894–1945

When Douglas Newbold embarked on his first journey of exploration in the Sudan in 1923, he already had some experience of the desert, having fought against the Turks in the Levant. It was there that he first became interested in archaeology, the desert, and nomads. After the war, in 1920, Newbold entered the Sudan Political Service. This adventurous classical scholar – a stocky man with mocking eyes under bushy black brows – preferred a camel saddle to an office chair, but his intellect and his sense of duty propelled him up the career ladder. In 1932 Douglas Newbold was appointed governor of North Kordofan, and in 1939 Civil Secretary. In the latter capacity he played an important role in the realization of an independent Sudan. 'A mere intellectual grasp of a country's physique will not, alone, engender a love of it,' wrote Newbold, who looked at Sudan with both his mind and his heart.

In 1923 he was a young administrator who listened mainly to his heart. *A Desert Odyssey of a Thousand Miles*, an account of his first survey by camel in North Kordofan, is an ode to the glory of sand and sky. In the years that followed he contributed numerous articles to *Sudan Notes and Records*. Flora, fauna, archaeology, geology – everything was grist to the mill of his enquiring mind. But Newbold's job was demanding, and after 1927 there was little time for travel or research. A sense of duty stifled the voice of his heart. 'The scenes and incidents on the march faded at the journey's end from memory's inward eye', Newbold wrote in the introduction to the somewhat dry and factual report of his 1927 survey trip to the uninhabited oasis of Nukheila,

The Blue Nile in Khartoum, Sudan, seen from Douglas Newbold's house. Newbold preferred the desert, but as a high-ranking administrator, he was tied to Khartoum.

Sudan, 1927. Douglas Newbold on his second great expedition across the Sudanese desert with his colleague Shaw and several nomads. Newbold poses with two baby cheetahs. One of his guides had shot the mother cheetah.

undertaken together with his colleague Kennedy-Shaw. It would be his last long desert trek and, being pressed for time, Newbold focused on the facts. 'We can only leave it to those who have passed many desert nights and days, to fill in with their imagination the colours of our monochrome picture.'

Seventy-seven years after Newbold travelled a thousand miles across the Sudanese desert to reach Atrun oasis, I undertook my first camel journey in North Darfur. I too wanted to visit Atrun, and in my saddlebag I kept a well-thumbed copy of *A Desert Odyssey of a Thousand Miles*. On the first page Newbold refers to the drawings of unicorns and dog-headed men with tails with which old mapmakers had decorated the maps of the area. Some had simply written across the expanse of wasteland: 'Here dwelle very eville men'. No monsters or devils appeared on my 60-year-old British map, but there were certainly enough empty spaces. Those expanses of white bore the spidery dotted lines which marked the routes followed by British scouts at the beginning of the last century. Two of those lines bear the name of Newbold, together with the dates 1923 and 1927.

Douglas Newbold left from Hamrat es Sheikh. I started my journey in El Fasher, but I calculated that I would be able to catch up with my predecessor at Zolat Hammad. This group of hills, with their numerous rock inscriptions, lies just forty kilometres southwest of Atrun oasis, and if I altered my course by a few degrees, I would pass very close to it.

Excitedly, I showed Yussuf Gamaa, my desert guide, Newbold's drawings of the inscriptions and the accompanying key map. He denied the existence of Zolat Hammad and refused to deviate from his intended course.

I swallowed my anger, realizing that it would be more prudently employed at the moment we reached the uninhabited oasis of Nukheila, which Yusuf was

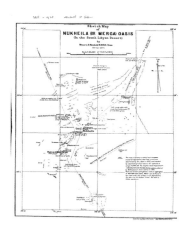

Map of the Nukheila oasis (also known as Merga), drawn during the 1927 expedition of Newbold and Shaw. The sketch is based on measurements carried out using a compass and a wheel that recorded distances.

likewise determined not to visit. In 1923 Douglas Newbold had also dreamed of this mysterious oasis where no European had ever set foot. 'It was a great disappointment to me that my instructions did not allow me to go on to it,' he wrote, after reaching the salt pans of Atrun. Nukheila oasis was only three days' march ahead, but the conscientious Newbold turned back. On November 27, 1927 he and Kennedy-Shaw did reach the salt lake in Nukheila, surrounded by palm trees. Newbold did not describe his emotions, but no doubt he rejoiced at the sight of the pool of blue water encircled by cream-coloured sand dunes in the middle of a no-man's land.

February 2000 I reached the fairy-tale oasis, and clutching Newbold's account, I found the rock carvings of cows, and scrambling over the enormous stone outcroppings, I was conscious of his presence. Standing on top of a rock, I felt a shiver at the sight of those undulating sand dunes, the yellow carpet that stretched from horizon to horizon. No doubt Douglas Newbold had also felt the presence of death when he stood on this very spot.

'In the desert,' he wrote, 'there is no fear except the fear of death, and where better to die than on the clean sand under the stars.'

His wish was not granted. Douglas Newbold died in Khartoum at the age of fifty.

Théodore Monod
1902—2000

'I dwell between my two oceans, the one I possess and the one I long for, the ocean of the ships and that of the dromedaries: uncertain, unresolved, torn apart,' wrote Théodore Monod of his first encounter with the desert.

He was a 22-year-old marine biology student and had just finished a study of saltwater fish in the coastal waters of Mauretania when he turned his gaze from salt water to sand. Théodore Monod joined a passing trade caravan, thereby changing the course of his career. Professor Monod was a scientist in the classic tradition of the nineteenth century. He was both a naturalist, someone who studies the existing situation, and a generalist, who regards botany, archaeology, geology, and geography as a natural part of his sphere of activity. His intellect, his adventurous mind-set, and his insatiable hunger for knowledge made him one of the greatest researchers the Sahara has ever known.

For twenty-five years from 1938 Prof. Monod headed the prestigious French Institute for Black Africa (IFAN) in Dakar, Senegal. His wife and children were accustomed to his departures on extended trips. Monod's Sahara expeditions lasted many months, and each time he returned with notebooks full of closely written pages and crates of stones, fossils, dried plants, and mounted insects.

He also charted the Majabat-al-Koubra, some 250,000 square kilometres of desert in the Western Sahara. In that waterless area, he survived on a litre a day.

Théodore Monod was driven by curiosity and by a desire to unravel the secrets of the Sahara, but his publications also

Travel account from 1934, with geological mapping and notes. The generalist Théodore Monod studied all the various aspects of nature.

Théodore Monod, Mauretania, 1955.

betray a yearning for quiet and contemplation. As a boy, he had considered following in a family tradition by studying theology. Things turned out differently, but where was he better able to experience the presence of God than in the Sahara?

Until his death the elderly Monod continued to travel the desert. He published his findings and spoke at scientific conferences. At home in Paris, he had his offices in the Muséum national d'Histoire naturelle; anyone wishing to speak to the busy professor had to make an appointment well in advance.

In 1994 I knocked on the door of his office for the first time. Nervous and timid, but also excited at the prospect of shaking hands with the great explorer of the Sahara.

The professor was waiting for me. His small, hunched form almost disappeared behind the immense desk, covered with papers, stone celts, screw-topped jars, plastic bags of stones, and shards of rare, dull-green Libyan glass, acquired during an expedition across the Great Sand Sea, in the borderland between Libya and Egypt. I had told Professor Monod that I wanted to talk to him about his expeditions in Sudan, my next destination. He had set aside a small pile of books and geographic maps, but I was far more interested in the person sitting opposite me.

Monod waved aside personal questions. He was first and foremost a scientist, and he did not appreciate people rooting around in his life. Facts, that's what the 92-year-old professor wanted to talk about.

Before I left he took me to his library. The shelves were filled with books on every conceivable aspect of the Sahara, many of them with a personal inscription. 'Why don't you take it along to copy?' he suggested when I pointed to a rare volume. *Unbekannte Sahara* (*Unknown Sahara*, 1939). It was written by the

Rock engravings in the Western Sahara, recorded by Monod in 1934.

Hungarian count Almásy, made famous by the film *The English Patient*, which was modelled on him. Back in 1994, the Hungarian explorer was virtually unknown and his book out of print.

During a second visit Professor Monod opened a filing cabinet containing the notebooks he'd kept on all his trips. I'd seen photos of the neatly covered notebooks, with their squared paper, but assumed that the originals were kept in a vault. Now I was holding one of the journals dating from 1934 and looking at the right-hand page, filled with the professor's round, flowing handwriting. The left-hand page was reserved for drawings and numbered finds.

When I left, I thanked the professor for taking the time to see an amateur like me. 'It's not only the big discoveries that contribute to our knowledge of the earth,' he replied generously. In our conversations, but also in his contacts with his biographers, Théodore was reticent about the influence of the desert on his spiritual life. And yet, in the midst of that immense void he must have experienced something that rose above the tangible and the earthly. In *Méharées* (1937), his most personal book, he wrote: 'What does he think about, the solitary pilgrim, exposed to a merciless sun, on top of a camel, pinned between earth and sky as on some exalted pillory? No doubt he meditates, ponders life, thinks about the mistakes he's made, perhaps he prays…?'

Théodore Monod had hoped to die in the desert. He passed away in Paris, but the desert came to him in the guise of a camel which, at a slow, rocking gait, accompanied the body of the professor to his last resting place.

Wilfred Thesiger
1910—2003

Thesiger appears ill at ease in this photo: it is the first time he has worn Arab dress. Like the Bedouins, he is barefoot. In hostile territory Thesiger had to ride rather than walk, for his enormous foot-print would be recognized immediately.

'The harder the life, the finer the people,' concluded the British explorer Wilfred Thesiger after he had crossed the Rub al-Khali, the great sand desert of the Arabian Peninsula. It was a place where the chances of survival were slim indeed, and it is characteristic of Wilfred Thesiger that the happiest years of his life were spent in such a god-forsaken spot. The seeds of Thesiger's wanderlust and his interest in 'primitive' tribes were sown in Abyssinia (Ethiopia), where his father was a British minister. Nomads wielding spears, wild animals, simple huts, and the exuberant outpourings of nature formed the décor in which he grew up. The transition to a bleak, cold England, where he attended public school, was highly traumatic for the young Thesiger, and he never really felt at home until he went up to Oxford.

Having completed his studies and taken part in an expedition to the land of the bloodthirsty Danakil in East Africa, the twenty-five-year-old Wilfred voluntee-red for the Sudan Civil Service. From 1935 to 1938 he served as assistant to the District Commissioner and traveled by camel across Darfur, upholding the law. Thesiger resigned from the Service when he was assigned to a desk job. In 1945 he left for the Arabian Peninsula, where he was charged with searching out the breeding grounds of locusts. The task entrusted to him was of secondary importance. Wilfred Thesiger's true goal was to distinguish himself as a traveler and to chart the Rub al-Khali, or Empty Quarter. For five years he crisscrossed the unexplored sandy desert together with his young guides bin Kabina and bin Ghabaisha, until he was forced to leave

Thesiger's comrades Salim bin Kabina and Salim bin Ghabaisha of the Rashid tribe, Oman, 1950.

the country for political reasons.

Wilfred Thesiger always regretted his departure, because it was in the vastness of Rub al-Khali that he found what he longed for: camaraderie, freedom, and peace of mind. He believed that the desert had a salubrious effect on the human psyche. He regarded the city, with all its conveniences and material excesses, as the cesspool of humanity.

Arabian Sands, the account of his travels across the Arabian Peninsula, is a swan song. Thesiger had already foreseen the decline of the nomadic culture he so admired, and he concluded with regret that he had contributed to that decline by charting the natural habitat of the desert dwellers.

Wilfred Thesiger embraced that hard life in a world dominated by men. He was just as derogatory about women as about 'the spoiling hand of progress.' His dislike of women had kept me from seeking out the man who shared my passion for the desert, but our paths crossed indirectly during my trips across Darfur. In the Meidob Mountains I ran into someone who in the 1930s had served as a scout for Thesiger, rounding up Barbary sheep for him when he came to hunt there. The ninety-year-old brother of the former Meidob king said 'We called him the lion-killer,' since Thesiger often came to their aid when a hungry lion was seen in the vicinity of a village. More stories did the rounds in Kutum, where Wilfred Thesiger had been posted. I learned that he was once called to order by one of his soldiers, who noticed a nervous tremor in his leg when he got a bead on a lion.

It was in late 2001 that I met the lion-killer in person, during a visit to England. A mutual acquaintance assured me that Wilfred Thesiger had mellowed with age and would be delighted to receive me.

The desert explorer, still ramrod-straight, was waiting for me at the entrance of the old people's home where he lived. I was nervous and I don't remember much about that first meeting,

From 1946 on, Salim bin Ghabaisha accompanied Thesiger on his travels throughout the southern part of the Arabian Peninsula. In the photo, bin Ghabaisha is carrying feed for the camels

except for his piercing eyes under brushy brows, and the blue veins on his hands. Hands that had once knocked out opponents in the boxing ring, fired rifles, and performed circumcisions in the wilderness. Those penetrating eyes had witnessed events that I could only read about in the history books. I met Wilfred Thesiger on two other occasions before his death in 2003. Our conversations invariably centred on his years in Darfur and the way the world had become un-recognizable since the days when he and his Leica recorded life in the desert.

Wilfred Thesiger has often been criticized for his aversion to progress and his overly romantic representation of the nomadic life. His critics felt that Western man had no right to declare the rest of the world a museum. Listening to Thesiger, I understood that what he deplored above all was the disappearance of a world in which he had been happy.

During my last visit, I asked Wilfred Thesiger whether he would have taken me, an experienced desert traveler, along with him on one of his journeys.

'No,' he answered, without hesitation.

'Why not?' I insisted.

The old man straightened his back. The friendly expression on his wrinkled face hardened and for an instant I saw in this elderly man the uncompromising macho who had conquered the Rub al-Khali.

'I couldn't have taken you along, because you are a woman,' he said.

The answer made me feel good. Old age and Alzheimer's had not quelled the spirit of the old explorer.

To understand the Sahara, one must travel in its past.

Henri J. Hugot

FARAFRA OASIS
October 15
Farafra oasis, south of hill Gunna South
10 km

October 16
Bir Dikka, water and palm tree
32 km
October 17
Dunes near Karawein
30 km

October 18
Karawein, water hole, desert fox
13 km

Farafra Oasis to Abu Simbel
October 15 – December 25 1990

October 21
Wadi Maqfi, water hole
35 km
October 222
Wadi Maqfi, going around in circles
October 23
Wadi Hennis, horned viper
23 km

October 28
South of Ain Tinin, stony
32 km

October 29
Across a wadi, near old caravan trail
26 km

October 30
Wadi, dry grass
27 km

October 31
Stony plateau, bad going
28 km
November 1
Valley, prehistoric pottery
18 km
November 2
Near cliff, searching for a way down
33 km
November 3
Charb el Mahoub, leave young camel Rashid behind
16 km
November 7
Sand dune
35 km
November 9
On the edge of my map
41 km

November 13
Near row of hills, behind it flat desert
40 km
November 14
Ain Amur, sandstone temple, brackish water
10 km
November 16
Sandstone hill with rock carvings and hieroglyphs
26 km
November 17
Umm Dabadibb, Roman fortress
15 km
November 19
Labakha, Roman fortress, good grazing
17 km
November 20
Windy gorge on plateau
27 km
December 10
South of Dush, Kharga Oasis, night walk
34 km
December 12
Nukheila, group of palm trees, tasty dates
41 km

December 15
Dungul North, vegetation, no water
42 km
December 16
Dungul South, small water hole
8 km
December 21
Tushka, arrested by army soldiers
30 km
December 24
South of Tushka
38 km
December 25
ABU SIMBEL

November 13
Midday break. Ancient wind shield along
caravan trail.

November 9
Plateau northwest of Dakhla oasis

Clouds float above the white limestone hills, into which the figures of giraffes have been scratched. On days like this, I feel joy simply because I exist.

February 5 (on the way back)
Camp at the bottom of Bab el Gasmund
pass

A sand slide makes it possible to descend from the plateau to Dakhla oasis. It is mid-afternoon and the shadows are creeping along the rocks and across the rolling sand in an upward direction. I camp at the foot of a sandy pass.

March 10 (on the way back)
Camp in the sand-hills

The Abu Muharik, a sand barrier between Bahariya and Kharga, is five kilometres wide and 125 kilometres long. The steep dunes are magnificent, but crossing them with camels is a terrifying experience.

November 3
On my way to the village of Charb el
Mahoub, Dakhla oasis.

It takes forever to cross the yardangs, wind-eroded clay hills, at the foot of a high limestone plateau bordering Dakhla oasis. I am heading for the village of Charb el Mahoub, where I hope to buy provisions and rest for a few days.

November 24
Camp in the desert north of Kharga

Flat terrain is a treat for camel feet. When the going is easy, I have time to search the desert floor for scrapers, spearheads and grinding stones left behind by the prehistoric people who lived here thousands of years ago.

November 14
Camp at Ain Amur

Ain Amur is a magical place, situated on a flat terrace halfway up a cliff which lies east of Kharga Oasis. Reeds surround a spring and there are palm trees. Caravans on their way from Dakhla to Kharga had to pass by the Roman toll house and the sandstone temple of Ain Amur.

November 2
In search of the pass leading into Dakhla
oasis

*The plateau between Farafra and Dakhla oasis
is awesome, but you have to know your way
around. In wind-still weather I camped on a
sand dune and wandered around in my bare
feet, taking in the silence.*

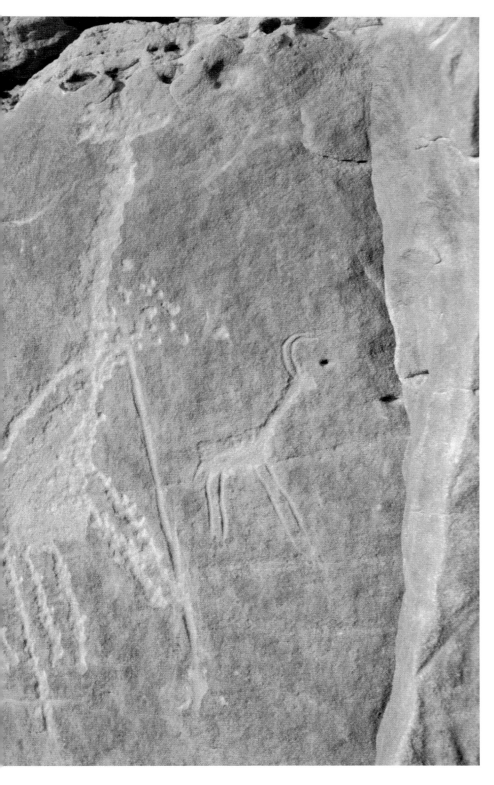

November 16
Camp at the foot of a sandstone hill with
rock carvings

*The sandstone outcropping bordering the trail
between Dakhla and Kharga used to be covered
with graffiti: giraffes, ostriches, gazelles,
hieroglyphs, sun boats, female figures, and
demotic script. Until a recent downpour wiped
out thousands of years of history.*

November 7
I make my camp on top of the cow
smugglers pass

*Smugglers use the sandy pass at Charb el
Mahoub in Dakhla oasis to guide cows to the
Nile Valley, thus avoiding the export tax.
Coming from higher ground, the pass is
difficult to find because of the wilderness of
wind-eroded hills atop the plateau.*

People—A sandstorm obscured the sky as I approached the wells of Abu Sofiyan in North Kordofan, Sudan. Unloading my camel, I saw movement in the wall of sand, and a little later a salt caravan appeared. Much to my surprise, since I had assumed that the camel as beast of burden had been replaced by the truck at least a decade ago. Within minutes the pack camels were divested of their heavy salt bags, and the camel drivers raced off to the nearest well to reserve a spot. After watering their thirsty animals, the men talked about the perilous journey they had just completed. This was in early 2004, when few dared approach the lucrative saltpans of Atrun, for fear of being attacked by rebels from neighbouring Darfur. These men had thrown caution to the wind, because their family was in urgent need of money. One man always served as a lookout, and though no one had appeared, the deathly silence was at least as frightening as a sudden sign of life. 'We made it,' said the leader Fadrallah Salih, concluding his account. 'Thanks to Allah.'

People—Arabiya was an imposing woman with a shrill voice and a cheeky attitude. She was also the uncrowned queen of Ain Tinin, an idyllic Egyptian oasis which, when I arrived in 1988, was home to two families.

Arabiya eclipsed everyone and bossed them around. She was quick to laugh, but if my gifts did not live up to her expectations, her voice took on a frosty edge. And I knew that during my absence she went through my luggage: a zipper would be torn and repaired with coarse stitches.

My admiration for the Egyptian matron waned: after a few trips I found other accommodations for my camels and expedition gear.

After that I seldom thought about Ain Tinin, until news of Arabiya's death reached me. Arabiya had witnessed the beginnings of my desert career, had watched me flounder and grow in my role as a caravan leader. True, she had been greedy, but she had also offered me a safe haven. Countless threads connected me with Arabiya, something which I didn't realize until her death severed all ties with the living past.

Places—The mummified child, whose face still bore traces of gold leaf, was just lying there in the sand. Grave robbers in search of treasure had removed the fragile body from its tomb, hewn out of a sandstone hill to the west of Ain Labakha. This Egyptian settlement, situated in the northwestern corner of Kharga Oasis, had once been a thriving Roman village.

A faintly acidic graveyard smell surrounded the child. Despite the fact that the little boy had been lying in a closed gravesite for at least fifteen hundred years, the face was intact, and I could count the fingers of his hands. From where I stood, I could distinguish the ruins of the rock-cut temple built in the reign of Antoninus Pius. The white plaster on a crumbling mud brick wall bore a painted image of the dwarf god Bes, a creature with deformed legs, the tail of a lion, and a mask-like face with the tongue sticking out. The ugly features of Bes were designed to ward off evil spirits, but for all his supposed power, the dwarf-god had not been able to save the beautiful child lying at my feet.

Places—From the fourth to the seventh century there were Christians living in the Egyptian oases of Dahkla and Kharga. I hadn't realized this until I discovered the remains of churches and monastaries in Kharga, the southernmost oasis. Initially I mistook the Monastery of Mustafa Kashif (photo) for a fort, until I came closer and saw a church half-buried under the sand, with Greek graffiti scrawled across its white plastered walls. The monastery dates from the fifth or sixth century, and those sturdy walls were calculated to repulse the Blemmyes, a desert folk from the far south of the country. But given the age of the nearby graves, this spot was in use as early as the fourth century.

I enjoyed camping out in this quiet and remote spot, searching the piles of potsherds for unusual specimens, or roaming through the countless chambers. In the middle of the day, the walls of church and monastery afforded at least a modicum of shadow. There I passed the hottest hours of each day, speculating on what convent life was like in that distant past.

Places—Opposite the entrance to the hidden valley with rock art in Nurayet, amid the Red Sea Hills of Sudan, stands the solitary Jebel Magardi. The setting sun brings that sombre pinnacle to life. A blood-red wave passes over the rocks, which seem to vibrate with excitement. When the sun disappears, the fire is extinguished and the magic is gone. Nurayet had a cultic character, observed my travel companion, the archaeologist Krzysztof Pluskota. In ancient times the landscape was gendered: mountains were equated with males and fertile valleys with females. In Nurayet these two aspects came together: inside the womb-like valley the early pastoralists had performed magic rituals to multiply their herds and flocks.

Most of the rock art on the boulders and the walls depicts cattle with big horns. Hunting scenes are also presented, along with elephants, gazelles and a rhinoceros. The styles and the varying colours of the patina indicate that the engravings were made in prehistory and over a considerable period of time.

The mosque, a perimeter of loose stones intended for nomads and travellers, is much more recent.

Let's go then!
Bring the camels!

Pierre Loti

death snapping at her heels. She will stay in Dongola for a month while the rest of the herd will be taken to Egypt by a new crew of men, next week.

The same afternoon, having rested briefly, Djemera and his men climb aboard an empty Toyota pickup together with the few humble things they own and take their leave without much ado. A light handshake, a perfunctory greeting and they are gone, dissolved in a cloud of dust.

The relatively cheap camel meat is in great demand in the lower-class areas of Egypt, as here in the Cairo neighbourhood Imbaba. The end product, meat for the retail market, provides the nomads of Sudan with a livelihood. Without camels, they would have no income.

Day 19~February 3~25 km~N 18.27.200 E 30.43.160
House of second trader.

Day 18~February 2~50 km~N 18.14.300 E 30.41.555
Lunch with the first trader. Banquet. Rode until 21:45.

Day 17~February 1~60 km ~N17.55.674 E 30.54.035
Irritation at the extremely long days in the saddle.

Day 16~January 31~60 km~N16 17.32.274 E 30.31.842
Sweltering. Back pain. Trotted until it got dark.

Day 15~January 30~45 km~N 17.06.750 E 30.16.707
Clouds in the sky. Smells. Camels limping.

Day 14~January 29~50 km~N 16.51.482 E 29.57.603
Diarrhoea. Camel tick in neck. Dead camel.

Day 13~January 28~50 km~N 16.33.500 E 29.34.167
Unbelievable: tea break at 10 o'clock. Donkey caravan spotted.

Day 12~January 27~50 km~N 16.22.894 E 29.14.625
Camels ate all night long. Three missing. Found.

Day 11~January 26~ 40 km~N 16.07.727 E 28.48.940
At the well in Wadi Millik. Faster, faster.

Day 10~January 25~50 km~N 15.51.619 E 28.14.495
Pa's birthday. Bloody cold night.

Day 9~January 24~50 km~N 15.30.000 E 28.26.205
No rest for the wicked. Ali has a hernia or something.

Day 8~January 23~40 km~N 15.11.943 E 28.12.774
Meeting with Kababish boys. Baby camel left behind.

January–February 2001
The 40 days road~El Fasher to Dongola

Day 7~January 22~45 km~N 14.55.000 E 28.00.889
No grass. Baobab. Hurry, hurry, hurry.

Day 6~January 21~46 km~N 14.37.119 E 27.50.073
Woke up to the sight of the Southern Cross.

Day 5~January 20~50 km~N 14.27.240 E 27.26.150
Soldiers take their leave. Limping camels.

Day 4~January 19~47 km~N 14.15.286 E 27.01.908
Rode all day, only a one-hour stop. Different riding camel.

Day 3~January 18~48 km ~N 14.05.927 E 26.35.727
Everyone has a cold. Pace a constant trot. Pain. Thank God for Yussuf.

Day 2~January 17~60 km~N 13.53.935 E 26.13.247
Knackered, broken. Country of thieves.

Day 1~January 16~41 km~N 13.41.664 E 25.47.092
Impossible tempo. Police want to see money.

Ten to thirteen hours per day in the saddle. The men kept up the pace, with loud cries and much cracking of whips.

Arrival near Debba on the Nile, on the eighteenth day. The camels slake their thirst at the house of one of the camel traders.

Text
Arita Baaijens

Photographs
Arita Baaijens, Carlo Bergmann: p.14, 16, 20, 26, 30, 31, 38.
Gerard Kooiman: p.84. Carl Maxwell: p.46. Aart Meijles:
p.30, 32, 35, 36, 75. Joanna B. Pinneo: back cover.
Krzysztof Pluskota: p.39. Photographic retouching cover image:
Marjan van Nus.

Picture editing
Reynoud Homan and Arita Baaijens

Design
Reynoud Homan

Translation
Barbara Fasting

Printed by
Veenman Drukkers, Rotterdam–NL

Author's Acknowledgements
Ahmed A. Fathallah, Carlo Bergmann, Niek Biegman, Lorraine
Chittock, Pat Clifford, Carol Ann Clouston, Nikolaos van Dam,
Samia Daoud, Yussuf Gamaa, Angela Homan, Charlotte
Huygens, Olaf Kaper, Gerard Kooiman, Fred Leemhuis,
Tjitske Lingsma, Carl Maxwell, Aart Meijles, Ambroise Monod,
Minka Nijhuis, Krzysztof Pluskota, Joanna B. Pinneo,
Fred Schmidt, Patrick Spijkerman, Erwin Tmmermans,
Will Tinnemans, Robert Twigger, Christine Wagner,
Maartje Wildeman, Wim van der Zwan.

With my special thanks to Gerrit Wildeman for his generous
support.

Picture credits
Frédéric Cailliaud
Collection Muséum d'histoire naturelle, © Patrick Jean,
Ville de Nantes.
  Gerhard Rohlfs
Rohlfs archive, Museum Schloss Schönebeck, Bremen.
Alexandrine Tinne: photographs from the Haags Gemeente-
archief collection, The Hague.
Map from De Constant Rebecque collection, Nationaal Archief,
The Hague.
  Rosita Forbes
photographs from *Appointed in the Sun* by Rosita Forbes, London:
Cassell, 1949. *Naar Koefara: Het Geheim van de Sahara* by Rosita
Forbes, Amsterdam, Querido, 1925.
  Douglas Newbold
photographs from the Durham University Library collection.
Map from *Sudan Notes and Records*, Vol XI, 1928.
  Théodore Monod
photographs from the private collection of the Monod family.
Rock engravings in the Western Sahara from *Méharées*, p.121 by
Théodore Monod, 1934, ed. 1937.
Notebook August December 1934, Théodore Monod collection,
Muséum national d'Histoire naturelle, Paris.
  Wilfred Thesiger
photographs from the Pitt Rivers Museum collection, University
of Oxford.

Quotes and poems
  Your camel is loaded to sing, p. 4
From: *The Gift: Poems by Hafiz the Great Sufi Master* translated by
Daniel Ladinsky, New York, Penguin, 1999, p.311.
  I was alone, p.15
From: *Wind, Sand and Stars* by Antoine de Saint-Exupéry, London
Picador, 1987, p.61.
  I am an old man, p.27
Poem from Somalia, collected by Ahmed Cali Abokor.
  Water, thou hast no taste, p.43
From: *Wind, Sand and Stars* by Antoine de Saint-Exupéry, London
Picador, 1987, p.114.
  The perfect journey, p. 37
From: *From Red Sea to Blue Nile: A Thousand Miles of Ethiopia* by
Rosita Forbes, London, Cassell & Co Ltd, 1925.
  To understand the Sahara, p. 76
From: *Zehntausend Jahre Sahara: Bericht über ein verlorenes Paradis* by
Henri J. Hugot und Maximilien Bruggman, Verlag C. J. Bucher,
1976.
  Delightful to the eye, p.99
From: *Arabia Deserta* by Charles M. Doughty, 1888.
From: *Passages from Arabia Deserta* selected by Edward Garnett, the
Life and Letters Series nr 21, London, Jonathan Cape Ltd, 1931.
  Let's go then, p.117
From: *The desert* by Pierre Loti; Salt Lake City, University of Utah
Press, 1993.

First published in Egypt in 2008 by
The American University in Cairo Press
113 Sharia Kasr el Aini, Cairo, Egypt
www.aucpress.com

This edition published by arrangement with Veenman Publishers

Copyright © 2008 by Veenman Publishers
Text copyright © 2008 by Arita Baaijens
Photography copyright © 2008 by Arita Baaijens, Carlo
Bergmann, Gerard Kooiman, Carl Maxwell, Aart Meijles,
Joanna B. Pinneo, Krzysztof Pluskota.

Dar el Kutub No. 8223/08
ISBN 978 977 416 211 4

Dar el Kutub Cataloging-in-Publication Data

Baaijens, Arita
    Desert Songs: The Desert of Egypt and Sudan through
the Eyes of a Woman Explorer / Arita Baaijens.– Cairo:
The American University in Cairo Press, 2008
    p.   cm.
    ISBN 977 416 211 0
    1. Egypt – Description and travel   2. Sudan – Description and travel   I. Title
    916

Printed in The Netherlands

www.arita.baaijens.com

BLANKETS / 4 BAGS FOR FODDER (OLD) / 4 WHITE WATER BAGS (23 LTR) / 2X 30 LTR WATER BAGS. BAGS LUGGAGE (4 + 3) / FLEECE SHEET / MEASURING CAN DRY FODDER / 3 BUCKETS / MUMMY SLEEPING BAG / 3 PROVISION BAGS / FOOD: 7 TUNA CANS, 2 CHEESE, 13 SOUP, PASTA, RICE, SOUTH AFRICAN TEA (3X), 3 X POTATO PUREE, KILO MUESLI, TIN BUTTER, BEEF CUBES, PARMESAN CHEESE GRATED, EGYPTIAN TEA, CUSTARD, COCOA, MINT TEA + TINS, BAG WITH CANDY. TO DO: NEW FODDER BAGS. FUNNEL. REPAIR ZIPPER. NEW WATER JERRYCAN. DRIED VEGETABLES. BANDAGE AND MEDICINES. LIST PROVISIONS. BINOCULARS SAYID. SMALL JERRYCAN FOR SPIRITUS (2 LTR) / CAROLANN. APRIL 2001 IN CAIRO: VIXEN BINOCULARS / BOOKS: ROHLFS. HIEROGLYPHS / BIRDS / ENG-ARAB DICTIONARY / PICTURES / COPY BOOK (EMPTY) / LARGE TOWEL / BLACK-WHITE DOTS TROUSERS / BLACK TROUSERS / WIDE / CITY TROUSERS / FLEECE TROUSERS, BLACK / DOWN JACKET / PHOTOGRAPHERS JACKET / MONEY BELT / SUNCREAM FACTOR 15 (BOTTLE) AND 30 AND 20 / RED BAG WITH COMPASS / PRESENTS / CEBE SUN GLASSES / SEWING NEEDLES (LARGE) / 2 PAIR OF SOCKS / MANY COTTON BAGS / SUN HAT / SHOULDER BAG FOR CAMEL SADDLE / 2 JELLABA TROUSERS / 1 JELLABA / WHITE TURBAN, LONG / COTTON SHAWL, HEAD / SWEDISH ARMY SHIRT / WARM SOCKS / SLIPPERS / STRONG SEWING THREAD / RUBBER BANDS / SRL / INJECTION NEEDLES CAMELS / 2 SETS NEEDLES HEMA / MIRROR / CALENDULAMILK / PAPER FOR ROLING CIGARETTES / LOTION FOR FACE / VITAMINS / COMPASS RUUD / NET AGAINST FLIES / RED SHAWL / 2 PAIR OF SOCKS FOR WALKING (WINNIE) / CAROLANN. JANUARY 2001. CAIRO. STAR CHART / CLOTHES / PURSE / CREDIT CARD / KEYS - AMSTERDAM / DUFFLE BAG / SADDLE BAG / UNDER THE BED: 4 WATER BUFFOLO HIDES / BOX WITH KEYS ETC. BOOKS TO TAKE TO HOLLAND / GREEN-WHITE BAG IN ATTIC AND SLEEPING BAG IN ALBERT HEYN BAG / DUFFLE BAG AND OTHER BAG LONG BLUE SKIRT / AFRICAN HOUSE DRESS / MONEY BELT / BLACK SHAWL / GREY JOGGING TROUSERS / COLOURFUL BLOUSE / ARMY SHIRT SWEDEN / PANTS AND JELLABY / GREEN ARMY SHIRT / WOOLEN CAP / LEITZ BINOCULARS / OINTMENT / STREPSILS / BOTTLE WITH VITAMINS / 1 LTR WATER FLASK / LISTS WORDS GERMAN / SUDANESE ARABIC / DUTCH POSTCARDS / QURAN / PLASTIC ZIP-LOCK BAGS, LARGE 10X / NOTEPAD, SMALL (2X) / MEDIUM (1X) / CHINESE DIARY (1X) / BLUW SUEDE SHOES / BLACK PUMPS / SLIPPERS / PHOTOGRAPHERS JACKET (TOO SMALL!) / CANDY FOR THROAT / TENT / PLASTIC CONTAINERS WITH TOP: ? LTR (3) / 1 LTR (1) / MUG / 2 X 30 LTR JERRYCAN / WALKING SHOES (GOOD) / FLEECE SHEET / RED SLEEPING BAG / GLOVES / RUBBER SLEEPING MAT (BLUE) / JERRYCAN SPIRITUS (EMPTY) / FUNNEL / JERRYCAN / SCOOP / KNIFE / SADDLE (COMPLETE) / LEATHER SADDLE GOURD (COMPLETE) / WHIP / LEATHER RASN / PROTECTION LEGS (HASKANIT) / TRIPOD / REFLECTION SHEET / INJECTION NEEDLES / AMPULS / TANGIA COOKING SET / WATER KETTLE / COTTON BAGS (3) / CONTAINER FOR SALT / MATCHES / STRONG RUBBER BANDS / 5 ZIPPERS FOR BAGS / PAIR OF PINCERS / MEASURING TAPE / RAZER BLADES / TAPE TO TIE UP COOKER / CANVAS CLOTH REPAIR / 2 BUNDLES WHITE ROPE / BLUE MEDICINE BAG WITH SHAMPO AGAINST LICE, DAMPO, VASELINE, TAPE, EYE DROPS, ASPERINES, OINTMENT CAMELS / 2 BROKEN WATER BAGS / BODY WARMER / HEAD BAND / DESINFECTION CAMELS / PENCILS / SHARPENER / LIGHT METER CAMERA – NEXT TRIP / BUY EXTRA PARTS FOR THE SADDLE / ORDER SADDLE CUSHIONS / OGAL / ROPE FOR THE HEAD AND NECK / ROPE TO TIE CAMELS IN AGOUL / FODDER BAGS 40X30 CM / BAGS FOR FODDER / JERRYCANS 5 LITRE / IVOMEC / INJECTION NEEDLES / AMPULLA / TAR TO TREAT CAMEL FEET / OINTMENT / DESINFECTION POWDER / SADDLE GOURTS! / LEATHER TO ENLARGE SADDLE BELT / CLIP BINDING SADDLE / SEWING NEEDLES, BIG / PLASTIC SHEET RAIN PROTECTION / MUSQUITO NET / PLASTERS / COTTON / REFLECTION SHEET / 18 MM LENS / SMALL TRIPOD / MOTORDRIVE / GOOD TRIPOD / WARM SLEEPING BAG / FOLD-UP BUCKETS / CLIPS TO CLOSE COTTON BAGS / THIMBLE / FILE / SAW / LEATHER BELTS FOR SADDLE 20 MM WIDE AND 50 CM LONG + EXTRA PIECE / ROPE TO TIE RUN-AWAY CAMELS / STORIES ABOUT STARS / INSULATION BAG FOR FILMS / MAKE-UP BAG / RUCKSACK CAMERA / LARGE FIRST AID KIT / LARGE SEWING KIT / MEASUREMENTS BAGS: 55X45X25 FOR JERRYCANS, 60X50 FODDER BAGS, 65X30X40 WATER BAG, 80X30X50 ROPE BAG / NAMES PHARAOS AND DYNASTIES / SKETCH BOOK, ALPHABET COPTIC, GREEK, DEMOTIC / HIEROGLYPHS / GAFFER TAPE / PENCILS / PLASTIC SHEETS / SPORT TAPE / SEWING THREAT SHOE MAKES / CANVAS / SMALL MIRROR – FEBRUARY 2006, ABLA, TUNIS IN FAYOUM (EGYPT): METAL BOX WITH FOOD, 8X 25 LTR JERRYCAN, 3X 5 LTR JERRYCAN FOR SPIRITUS (2 EMPTY, 1 FULL), 2 BOXES COCOA, 13